Introdu

Beginning Your 30-Day Path into Shadow Work

Welcome to an illuminating journey of self-discovery! Shadow work is an incredible practice that involves introspection and integration of the parts of ourselves that we often hide or deny the aspects that we consider negative, unwanted, or shameful. This journal is designed to help you on a daily basis to reflect and explore your shadow self, allowing you to embrace and heal these hidden elements. Let's begin this journey of transformation together!

To start your 30-day path to shadow work, find a quiet and comfortable space where you can dedicate some time to yourself daily. Set an intention for your practice - this could be anything from gaining self-awareness, healing past traumas, or simply becoming more accepting of yourself.

Each day, take some time to reflect on your thoughts, feelings, and behaviors. Try to identify patterns and triggers that may be connected to your shadow self. Write down your observations in this journal and allow yourself to be honest and vulnerable.

As you progress through this journey, you may notice some resistance or discomfort as you confront certain aspects of yourself. This is completely normal and part of the healing process. Remember to practice self-compassion and kindness towards yourself throughout the journey.

By the end of the 30 days, you may find that you have gained a greater sense of self-awareness and acceptance. Embracing your shadow self can lead to a more authentic and fulfilling life. Congratulations on taking the first step towards your transformation!

Daily Check-in

DATE _____   S M T W T F

TODAY I APPRECIATE:

_____
_____
_____
_____
_____
_____
_____
_____

WATER IN TAKE:

◊ ◊ ◊ ◊ ◊ ◊ ◊ ◊ ◊ ◊

MY FAVOURITE AFFIRMATIONS FOR TODAY:

_____
_____
_____
_____
_____
_____
_____
_____

Day 1: Identifying Shadows

Examining Your Negative Self-Perceptions: Confronting a Personal Flaw

Take a moment to reflect on a quality you possess that you frequently criticize or feel embarrassed about. Describe this characteristic in detail and recognize its impact on your life. Reflect on any past experiences or beliefs that may have influenced the development of this negative perception.

Once you have identified and described this characteristic, it's time to confront and challenge the negative self-perception. Ask yourself if this flaw is really as significant as you believe it to be, or if it's simply a distorted view of reality. Consider how this perception is affecting your life and relationships, and whether it's preventing you from achieving your goals and potential.

It's important to challenge the negative self-talk that may arise when thinking about this flaw. Instead of criticizing yourself, try to reframe the way you think about the characteristic. For example, if you tend to be overly critical of yourself for being shy, try to view it as a personality trait rather than a flaw. Embrace your uniqueness and recognize that everyone has their own set of strengths and weaknesses.

Finally, make a conscious effort to practice self-compassion and kindness towards yourself. Remember that nobody is perfect, and it's okay to have flaws and make mistakes. Celebrate your strengths and accomplishments, and strive to improve in areas that you feel could use some work. With time and effort, you can learn to accept and even appreciate the things that make you unique, flaws and all.

Day 1: Identifying Shadows

EXAMINING YOUR NEGATIVE SELF-PERCEPTIONS: CONFRONTING A PERSONAL FLAW

Reflect on one quality of yourself that you often criticize or feel ashamed of. Describe this quality and acknowledge its presence in your life. Write about any past experiences or beliefs that contributed to the development of this shadow.

_____

_____

_____

_____

_____

_____

_____

_____

_____

_____

_____

Daily Check-in

DATE _____ S M T W T F

TODAY I APPRECIATE:

_____
_____
_____
_____
_____
_____
_____

WATER IN TAKE:

◊ ◊ ◊ ◊ ◊ ◊ ◊ ◊ ◊ ◊

MY FAVOURITE AFFIRMATIONS FOR TODAY:

_____
_____
_____
_____
_____
_____

Day 2: Understanding Origin

EXPLORING YOUR SHADOW: REFLECT ON YOUR SHADOW'S
ORIGIN AND IMPACT

When reflecting on your shadow, it's important to consider where it comes from. Was it shaped by childhood experiences, societal conditioning, or specific events? Take some time to think about the moments or factors that may have contributed to its formation. Additionally, reflect on how your shadow has affected your life so far.

Once you have identified the origins of your shadow, it's time to work on integrating it. This involves acknowledging and accepting the parts of yourself that you may have been repressing or denying. It's important to remember that everyone has a shadow, and it's a natural part of being human. By integrating your shadow, you can gain a deeper understanding of yourself and your motivations, leading to greater personal growth and fulfillment. It may be helpful to seek the guidance of a therapist or counselor to support you in this process. Remember, embracing your shadow is a courageous act that can lead to a more authentic and fulfilling life.

As you work on integrating your shadow, it's important to practice self-compassion and patience. Integrating your shadow is not a quick fix, but rather a lifelong journey. It may also be challenging and uncomfortable at times, as you confront parts of yourself that you may have been avoiding. However, the rewards of this process are worth it. By integrating your shadow, you can experience greater self-awareness, self-acceptance, and inner peace. So take your time, be gentle with yourself, and trust in the process.

Day 2: Understanding Origin

Explore the origin of your identified shadow. Was it influenced by childhood experiences, societal conditioning, or specific events? Write about the moments or factors that may have contributed to its formation. Reflect on how it has impacted your life so far.

_____

_____

_____

_____

_____

_____

_____

_____

_____

_____

_____

Daily Check-in

DATE _____   S M T W T F

TODAY I APPRECIATE:

_____
_____
_____
_____
_____
_____
_____
_____

WATER IN TAKE:

◊ ◊ ◊ ◊ ◊ ◊ ◊ ◊ ◊ ◊

MY FAVOURITE AFFIRMATIONS FOR TODAY:

_____
_____
_____
_____
_____
_____
_____

Day 3: Embracing Compassion

As you delve deeper into your shadow, practice self-compassion. Writing a letter of compassion to yourself can be a helpful tool. Address the aspect of yourself that embodies the shadow quality, and offer yourself kindness, understanding, and reassurance.

Rather than trying to suppress or ignore it, embracing and accepting it can lead to personal growth and healing. By acknowledging and showing compassion to the parts of ourselves that we may not like, we can begin to integrate them into our overall identity. This can lead to a greater sense of wholeness and authenticity. So take the time to explore your shadow self with kindness and compassion, and see where it leads you on your journey of self-discovery.

When exploring your shadow self, it's also important to create a safe space for yourself to do so. This may include setting boundaries with others or taking time to reflect and process your emotions. It's okay to seek support from a therapist or trusted friend as you navigate this journey.

Additionally, as you become more aware of your shadow self, you may notice patterns or habits that no longer serve you. Take the time to reflect on these and consider making changes that align with your values and goals. This may involve setting new intentions or creating healthy habits to replace old ones.

Day 3: Embracing Compassion

Practice self-compassion as you delve deeper into your shadow. Write a compassionate letter to yourself, addressing the part of you that embodies this shadow quality. Offer kindness, understanding, and reassurance to yourself.

_____

_____

_____

_____

_____

_____

_____

_____

_____

_____

_____

_____

_____

Daily Check-in

DATE _____ S M T W T F

TODAY I APPRECIATE:

_____
_____
_____
_____
_____
_____
_____
_____

WATER IN TAKE:

◊ ◊ ◊ ◊ ◊ ◊ ◊ ◊ ◊ ◊

MY FAVOURITE AFFIRMATIONS FOR TODAY:

_____
_____
_____
_____
_____
_____
_____

Day 4: Trigger Awareness

Take note of the triggers that activate your shadow quality. Observe how situations, people, or events tend to bring out this aspect of yourself. Look for common patterns and analyze why these triggers have such a hold on you.

Once you have identified your triggers, it's time to work on managing them. This can involve a variety of techniques such as mindfulness, self-reflection, and seeking support from others. It's important to remember that shadow qualities are a natural part of being human and everyone has them. By acknowledging and addressing them, we can learn to accept ourselves more fully and become more well-rounded individuals. So take the time to explore your shadow, and don't be afraid to seek help or guidance along the way.

One technique for managing shadow qualities is mindfulness, which involves being present in the moment and non-judgmentally observing our thoughts and feelings. This can help us recognize when our shadow is being triggered and allow us to respond in a more conscious and intentional way.

Self-reflection is another powerful tool for managing our shadow. By taking time to reflect on our experiences and emotions, we can gain insight into the underlying causes of our shadow qualities. This can help us develop strategies for addressing these triggers and managing our responses.

Day 4: Trigger Awareness

EXPLORING YOUR SHADOW: UNDERSTANDING YOUR TRIGGERS

Observe the triggers that activate your shadow quality. Reflect on situations, people, or events that tend to bring out this aspect of yourself. Identify common patterns and explore why these triggers have such power over you.

_____

_____

_____

_____

_____

_____

_____

_____

_____

_____

_____

Daily Check-in

DATE _____   S M T W T F

TODAY I APPRECIATE:

_____
_____
_____
_____
_____
_____
_____
_____

WATER IN TAKE:

◊ ◊ ◊ ◊ ◊ ◊ ◊ ◊ ◊ ◊

MY FAVOURITE AFFIRMATIONS FOR TODAY:

_____
_____
_____
_____
_____
_____
_____
_____

Day 5: Challenging Beliefs

EXPLORING YOUR SHADOW: ANALYZING THE BELIEFS AND ASSUMPTIONS OF YOUR SHADOW TRAIT

Take a closer look at the beliefs and assumptions surrounding your shadow trait. Ask yourself whether these beliefs are accurate or self-imposed. Assess their validity and try to approach them from different perspectives to challenge your current beliefs.

By acknowledging and owning our shadow traits, we can learn to integrate them into our personalities in a healthy and constructive way. This can lead to greater self-awareness, self-acceptance, and ultimately, greater personal growth and fulfillment. Remember, we are all multifaceted individuals, and our shadow traits are just one aspect of who we are. Embrace your whole self, including your shadow, and you may be surprised at the positive changes that can result.

It's important to note that embracing your shadow traits doesn't mean that you have to act on them in harmful ways. Rather, it means acknowledging their existence and learning to manage them in a healthy way. For example, if your shadow trait is a tendency towards anger, rather than suppressing it or lashing out, you can learn to recognize and address the underlying emotions that trigger your anger. This can lead to more constructive ways of expressing yourself and a greater sense of emotional balance.

Day 5: Challenging Beliefs

EXPLORING YOUR SHADOW: ANALYZING THE BELIEFS AND
ASSUMPTIONS OF YOUR SHADOW TRAIT

Examine the beliefs and assumptions associated with
your shadow quality. Are these beliefs accurate or self-
imposed? Question their validity and explore
alternative perspectives that challenge these beliefs.

_____

_____

_____

_____

_____

_____

_____

_____

_____

_____

_____

_____

Daily Check-in

DATE _____   S M T W T F

TODAY I APPRECIATE:

_____
_____
_____
_____
_____
_____
_____
_____

WATER IN TAKE:

◊ ◊ ◊ ◊ ◊ ◊ ◊ ◊ ◊ ◊

MY FAVOURITE AFFIRMATIONS FOR TODAY:

_____
_____
_____
_____
_____
_____
_____

Day 6: Integration Visualization

HARNESSING THE POWER OF VISUALIZATION TO INTEGRATE YOUR SHADOW SELF

Take a moment, close your eyes and visualize the integration of your shadow quality into your entire being. Envision this aspect of yourself merging with your strengths and virtues. As you do this, pay attention to any emotions or sensations that come up.

Allow yourself to fully feel and experience these emotions and sensations without judgment or resistance. This integration process can be challenging and uncomfortable at times, but it is essential for personal growth and self-awareness. Remember that your shadow qualities are not something to be ashamed of, but rather a natural part of being human. By embracing and integrating them, you can become a more whole and authentic version of yourself. Take your time with this visualization exercise and trust that the process will unfold naturally. When you feel ready, slowly open your eyes and take a deep breath in and out. Carry this sense of integration and acceptance with you throughout your day.

As you move forward, continue to acknowledge and accept all parts of yourself. Remember that your shadow qualities are not something to be suppressed or ignored, but rather an opportunity for growth and transformation. By integrating these aspects of yourself, you can become more self-aware and compassionate towards others. It's important to practice self-care and self-compassion throughout this process, as it can be difficult and emotional. Give yourself grace and patience as you work towards becoming a more whole and authentic version of yourself. With time and practice, this integration will become more natural and seamless. Remember to check in with yourself regularly and continue to embrace all aspects of your being.

Day 6: Integration Visualization

Close your eyes and visualize yourself integrating your shadow quality into your whole being. Imagine this aspect of yourself integrated with your strengths and virtues. Note any emotions or sensations that arise during this visualization.

_____

_____

_____

_____

_____

_____

_____

_____

_____

_____

_____

_____

Daily Check-in

DATE _____   S   M   T   W   T   F

TODAY I APPRECIATE:

_____
_____
_____
_____
_____
_____
_____
_____

WATER IN TAKE:

⬤ ⬤ ⬤ ⬤ ⬤ ⬤ ⬤ ⬤ ⬤ ⬤

MY FAVOURITE AFFIRMATIONS FOR TODAY:

_____
_____
_____
_____
_____
_____
_____

Day 7: Journal Prompt Break

Take some time to ponder and write about your insights, challenges, and emotions that have emerged during the first week of shadow work. It's important to reflect on your personal growth and development.

_____

_____

_____

_____

_____

_____

_____

_____

_____

_____

_____

Daily Check-in

DATE _____   S M T W T F

TODAY I APPRECIATE:

_____
_____
_____
_____
_____
_____
_____
_____

WATER IN TAKE:

◊ ◊ ◊ ◊ ◊ ◊ ◊ ◊ ◊ ◊

MY FAVOURITE AFFIRMATIONS FOR TODAY:

_____
_____
_____
_____
_____
_____
_____
_____

Day 8: Healing the Inner Child

Take a moment to reflect on the influence of your shadow quality on your inner child. Write a letter to your younger self, acknowledging any pain they may have experienced, while reminding them of your love and continued support. Additionally, offer a message of forgiveness for any self-blame related to your shadow aspect.

Acknowledging the impact of our shadow qualities on our inner child can be a powerful step towards healing and growth. It can be difficult to confront the pain and hurt that our younger selves may have experienced, but writing a letter to that child version of ourselves can be a transformative exercise.

As you write this letter, remember to be kind and compassionate towards that younger self. Acknowledge any struggles they may have faced, and remind them of the love and support that you have for them now. It can be helpful to offer a message of forgiveness for any self-blame or shame related to your shadow aspect. Remember that you are not defined by your past mistakes or flaws, and that growth and healing are always possible. Take this opportunity to offer yourself the love and understanding that you deserve, and to nurture the inner child within you.

Day 8: Healing the Inner Child

UNDERSTANDING THE CONNECTION BETWEEN YOUR INNER CHILD AND SHADOW QUALITY

Explore how your inner child is impacted by your shadow quality. Write a letter to your inner child, acknowledging their pain and reassuring them of your love and support. Offer forgiveness for any self-blame associated with this shadow aspect.

_____

_____

_____

_____

_____

_____

_____

_____

_____

_____

_____

Daily Check-in

DATE _____   S M T W T F

TODAY I APPRECIATE:

_____
_____
_____
_____
_____
_____
_____
_____

WATER IN TAKE:

◊ ◊ ◊ ◊ ◊ ◊ ◊ ◊ ◊ ◊

MY FAVOURITE AFFIRMATIONS FOR TODAY:

_____
_____
_____
_____
_____
_____
_____
_____

Day 9: Expressive Outlet

DISCOVER YOUR SHADOW SIDE THROUGH CREATIVE EXPRESSION

Ready to take a peek into your shadow side? Unleash your inner artist with painting, writing, dancing, or any other outlet that speaks to you. It's a way to bring those bottled up emotions to the surface and let them fly free. Don't hold back – give yourself permission to le your creativity run wild!

Exploring your shadow self can be a deeply rewarding and transformative experience. It allows you to confront and work through the parts of yourself that you may have been avoiding or suppressing. By tapping into your creativity, you can express and release these emotions in a healthy and productive way. This can lead to increased self-awareness, self-acceptance, and a greater sense of inner peace. So why not give it a try? Grab a canvas, a journal, or simply put on some music and let yourself get lost in the moment. You may be surprised at what you discover about yourself along the way.

It's important to approach this with self-compassion and patience. Don't judge yourself or your creations – instead, view them as a reflection of your unique journey and experiences. Additionally, don' feel like you have to do this alone. Consider enlisting the help of a therapist or trusted friend to guide you through the process and provide support along the way. With dedication and an open mind, exploring your shadow self can be a powerful tool for personal growth and healing.

Day 9: Expressive Outlet

DISCOVER YOUR SHADOW SIDE THROUGH CREATIVE EXPRESSION

Choose a creative outlet to express your shadow aspect. Paint, write, dance, or engage in any form of creative expression to externalize and release the emotions associated with this aspect. Allow yourself to express freely.

Daily Check-in

DATE _____   S M T W T F

TODAY I APPRECIATE:

_____
_____
_____
_____
_____
_____
_____
_____

WATER IN TAKE:

◇ ◇ ◇ ◇ ◇ ◇ ◇ ◇ ◇ ◇

MY FAVOURITE AFFIRMATIONS FOR TODAY:

_____
_____
_____
_____
_____
_____
_____

Day 10: Boundaries & Assertiveness

DEVELOPING BETTER RELATIONSHIPS THROUGH SELF-REFLECTION & ASSERTIVE COMMUNICATION

Take a moment to examine how your shadow quality is impacting your relationships, self-worth, and boundaries. Consider ways to communicate your needs assertively while still maintaining healthy boundaries. Take some time to reflect and jot down any adjustments you would like to make.

It's important to recognize that your shadow quality can affect more than just your own thoughts and emotions. It can also have a significant impact on your relationships with others. For example, if you struggle with feelings of jealousy or insecurity, this may cause you to act in ways that are damaging to your relationships. It's important to work on these issues and communicate your needs in a healthy and assertive way.

One way to do this is to focus on maintaining healthy boundaries. This means being clear about your own needs and limits, and communicating them effectively to others. It's okay to say no when you need to, or to ask for what you want in a respectful and assertive way. By setting and maintaining healthy boundaries, you can build stronger relationships with others and improve your own self-worth.

Take some time to reflect on your own shadow quality and how it may be impacting your life. Consider writing down any adjustments you would like to make, and think about how you can communicate your needs in a healthy and positive way. With patience, practice, and self-reflection, you can work towards a more fulfilling and satisfying life.

Day 10: Boundaries & Assertiveness

DEVELOPING BETTER RELATIONSHIPS THROUGH SELF-REFLECTION & ASSERTIVE COMMUNICATION

Reflect on how your shadow quality affects your relationships, self-worth, and boundaries. Explore ways to assertively communicate your needs while maintaining healthy boundaries. Write about any adjustments you'd like to make.

_____

_____

_____

_____

_____

_____

_____

_____

_____

_____

_____

_____

Daily Check-in

DATE _____   S M T W T F

TODAY I APPRECIATE:

_____
_____
_____
_____
_____
_____
_____
_____

WATER IN TAKE:

◊ ◊ ◊ ◊ ◊ ◊ ◊ ◊ ◊ ◊

MY FAVOURITE AFFIRMATIONS FOR TODAY:

_____
_____
_____
_____
_____
_____
_____

Day 11: Self-Forgiveness

EMBRACE GROWTH AND TRANSFORMATION BY PRACTICING SELF-FORGIVENESS

If you have made decisions or taken actions in the past that were influenced by your shadow aspect, it's important to practice self-forgiveness. A helpful exercise is to write a letter to yourself, acknowledging the past and forgiving yourself for any mistakes made. This can be a powerful tool for personal growth and transformation.

Self-forgiveness is not an easy task, but it is an essential step towards healing and moving forward. It's important to remember that we all have a shadow aspect and that making mistakes is a natural part of the human experience. By acknowledging our past actions and taking responsibility for them, we can learn from them and make better choices in the future.

Another helpful exercise is to practice self-compassion. This involves treating ourselves with the same kindness, understanding, and support that we would offer to a close friend or loved one. By cultivating self-compassion, we can develop a more positive and loving relationship with ourselves, which can lead to greater happiness and fulfillment in life.

Remember, self-forgiveness and self-compassion are ongoing practices. Be patient and gentle with yourself as you navigate your journey towards personal growth and transformation.

Day 11: Self-Forgiveness

EMBRACE GROWTH AND TRANSFORMATION BY PRACTICING SELF-FORGIVENESS

Practice self-forgiveness for any actions or decisions that were influenced by your shadow aspect. Write a letter forgiving yourself and embracing the opportunity for growth and transformation.

_____

_____

_____

_____

_____

_____

_____

_____

_____

_____

_____

_____

Daily Check-in

DATE _____   S M T W T F

TODAY I APPRECIATE:

_____
_____
_____
_____
_____
_____
_____
_____

WATER IN TAKE:

⬭ ⬭ ⬭ ⬭ ⬭ ⬭ ⬭ ⬭ ⬭ ⬭

MY FAVOURITE AFFIRMATIONS FOR TODAY:

_____
_____
_____
_____
_____
_____
_____

Day 12: Seek Support

EXPLORING YOUR SHADOW WORK: SEEKING HELP FROM A THERAPIST, COACH, OR TRUSTED FRIEND

If you're struggling with your shadow work, don't hesitate to seek assistance from a therapist, coach, or reliable friend. Document any concerns or doubts you may have and develop a strategy to seek support if needed.

Shadow work can be a challenging process, and it's important to remember that it's okay to ask for help. Seeking assistance from a professional or trusted confidant can provide you with valuable insights and help you navigate through difficult emotions. Writing down your thoughts and feelings can also be a helpful tool in identifying patterns and working towards healing. Remember, you don't have to go through your shadow work journey alone. There are resources and people available to support you every step of the way.

It's also important to approach your shadow work with compassion and understanding. It's natural to feel resistance or discomfort when delving into your shadow self, but try to avoid judging yourself for any negative emotions that may come up. Remember that shadow work is a process of self-discovery and growth, and it takes time and patience to fully integrate all aspects of yourself. Be kind and gentle with yourself throughout the process, and remember that healing is a journey, not a destination. With the right support and mindset, you can overcome any challenges that arise during your shadow work and emerge as a stronger, more whole version of yourself.

Day 12: Seek Support

Consider seeking support from a therapist, coach, or trusted friend who can help you navigate your shadow work. Write about any concerns or hesitations you may have and create a plan to seek support if necessary.

_____

_____

_____

_____

_____

_____

_____

_____

_____

_____

_____

Daily Check-in

DATE _____ S M T W T F

TODAY I APPRECIATE:

_____
_____
_____
_____
_____
_____
_____

WATER IN TAKE:

◊ ◊ ◊ ◊ ◊ ◊ ◊ ◊ ◊ ◊

MY FAVOURITE AFFIRMATIONS FOR TODAY:

_____
_____
_____
_____
_____
_____
_____

Day 13: Letting Go

EMBRACING YOUR SHADOW SELF: A LETTER OF RELEASE

Have you ever considered how freeing it would be to let go of the shame, guilt, or negativity associated with your shadow quality? Take a moment to reflect on it and write a letter to yourself. Describe the liberation and freedom you will experience when you release and integrate this aspect of yourself.

Letting go of the shame, guilt, or negativity that comes with our shadow qualities can be a life-changing experience. It's not easy to face and integrate the parts of ourselves that we may perceive as negative or undesirable, but it's essential for our growth and well-being.

In your letter to yourself, describe the feeling of liberation and freedom that you will experience when you finally release and integrate your shadow quality. Imagine how it would feel to no longer carry the weight of shame or guilt around with you.

Visualize yourself living life without this burden, and think about all the opportunities that will open up for you as a result. When we release and integrate our shadow qualities, we become more whole and authentic, and we are better able to connect with others in a meaningful way.

So, take a deep breath and let go of any fear or resistance you may be feeling. Write that letter to yourself and start the process of releasing and integrating your shadow quality. The freedom and liberation you will experience are well worth the effort.

Day 13: Letting Go

EMBRACING YOUR SHADOW SELF: A LETTER OF RELEASE

Reflect on what it would feel like to release the shame, guilt, or negativity associated with your shadow quality. Write a letter to yourself describing the freedom and liberation you will experience when you release and integrate this aspect.

_____

_____

_____

_____

_____

_____

_____

_____

_____

_____

_____

_____

Daily Check-in

DATE _____   S M T W T F

TODAY I APPRECIATE:

_____
_____
_____
_____
_____
_____
_____
_____

WATER IN TAKE:

◊ ◊ ◊ ◊ ◊ ◊ ◊ ◊ ◊ ◊

MY FAVOURITE AFFIRMATIONS FOR TODAY:

_____
_____
_____
_____
_____
_____
_____

Day 14: Journal Prompt Break

Reflect on your progress so far, any shifts in perception, or any challenges you've faced during the second week of shadow work.

_____

_____

_____

_____

_____

_____

_____

_____

_____

_____

_____

Daily Check-in

DATE _____   S M T W T F

TODAY I APPRECIATE:

_____
_____
_____
_____
_____
_____
_____
_____

WATER IN TAKE:

⬭ ⬭ ⬭ ⬭ ⬭ ⬭ ⬭ ⬭ ⬭ ⬭

MY FAVOURITE AFFIRMATIONS FOR TODAY:

_____
_____
_____
_____
_____
_____
_____

Day 15: Gratitude for Shadows

EMBRACING GROWTH AND WISDOM FROM SHADOW ASPECTS

Take some time to express gratitude for the shadows in your life. Consider the ways in which they have contributed to your personal development, and make a list of the lessons they've taught you. By embracing these experiences, you'll continue to grow and gain wisdom.

Shadows are often associated with negativity, but they can actually be valuable teachers. Without shadows, we wouldn't be able to appreciate the light. Similarly, without difficult experiences, we wouldn't be able to fully appreciate the good times. By acknowledging and learning from our shadows, we become better equipped to handle future challenges. So take some time to reflect on the shadows in your life and the lessons they've taught you. You may be surprised at how much you've grown as a result of these experiences. Remember, every shadow has a silver lining.

In the end, it's all about perspective. Shadows can be seen as obstacles or as opportunities for growth. By choosing to see them as the latter, we open ourselves up to a world of possibilities and personal development. So take some time today to reflect on the shadows in your life and the ways in which they've helped you become the person you are today. You may be surprised at how much you have to be grateful for.

Day 15: Gratitude for Shadows

EMBRACING GROWTH AND WISDOM FROM SHADOW ASPECTS

Express gratitude for the wisdom and growth your shadows have brought into your life. Write a list of ways your shadow aspects have contributed to your personal development. Embrace the lessons learned.

_____

_____

_____

_____

_____

_____

_____

_____

_____

_____

_____

_____

Daily Check-in

DATE _____   S M T W T F

TODAY I APPRECIATE:

_____
_____
_____
_____
_____
_____
_____
_____

WATER IN TAKE:

◊ ◊ ◊ ◊ ◊ ◊ ◊ ◊ ◊ ◊

MY FAVOURITE AFFIRMATIONS FOR TODAY:

_____
_____
_____
_____
_____
_____
_____

Day 16: Shadow Archetypes

UNDERSTANDING SHADOW ARCHETYPES FOR PERSONAL GROWTH

Have you ever heard of shadow archetypes? Take the time to research the various archetypes that relate to your shadow aspect. By doing so, you can gain a deeper understanding of yourself and start the healing process around your shadow quality.

The concept of shadow archetypes is rooted in the work of Carl Jung, a renowned Swiss psychiatrist and psychoanalyst. In his theory, Jung believed that the psyche is made up of both the conscious and unconscious mind. The conscious mind is what we are aware of, while the unconscious mind consists of repressed thoughts, emotions, and memories.

Jung believed that our shadow aspect is made up of the things we hide from ourselves and others. These could be negative traits, emotions, or experiences that we are ashamed of or fear being judged for.

Exploring shadow archetypes can be a powerful tool in understanding and integrating our shadow aspects. By identifying the archetypes that relate to our shadow, we can gain insight into the underlying causes of our negative patterns and behaviors. This can help us to heal and grow as individuals.

Some common shadow archetypes include the victim, the addict, the saboteur, and the dark magician. Each archetype represents a different aspect of our shadow, and by exploring them, we can gain a deeper understanding of ourselves and our behaviors.

Day 16: Shadow Archetypes

UNDERSTANDING SHADOW ARCHETYPES FOR PERSONAL GROWTH

Explore the concept of shadow archetypes. Research different archetypes that align with your shadow aspect. Reflect on how understanding these archetypes can deepen your understanding and healing around your shadow quality.

_____

_____

_____

_____

_____

_____

_____

_____

_____

_____

_____

_____

Daily Check-in

DATE _____   S M T W T F

TODAY | APPRECIATE:

_____
_____
_____
_____
_____
_____
_____

WATER IN TAKE:

◊ ◊ ◊ ◊ ◊ ◊ ◊ ◊ ◊ ◊

MY FAVOURITE AFFIRMATIONS FOR TODAY:

_____
_____
_____
_____
_____
_____
_____

Day 17: Mindfulness in the Shadows

DEVELOP MINDFULNESS AND LIVE IN THE PRESENT WHEN CONFRONTING YOUR SHADOW SELF

When your shadow self emerges, practice mindfulness and present moment awareness. Notice its presence without any judgment or attachment. Afterwards, reflect on any new insights or observations you may have gained from this practice by writing them down.

It is important to acknowledge that everyone has a shadow self, which represents the parts of ourselves that we may not be proud of or may be in denial about. However, it is crucial to confront and address our shadow self in order to grow and evolve as individuals. By practicing mindfulness and present moment awareness, we can learn to observe our shadow self without allowing it to control our actions or emotions. This can lead to valuable insights and self-awareness that can help us address any negative patterns or behaviors in our lives. By taking the time to reflect on these observations, we can begin to make positive changes and move towards a more fulfilling and authentic life.

Day 17: Mindfulness in the Shadows

DEVELOP MINDFULNESS AND LIVE IN THE PRESENT WHEN
CONFRONTING YOUR SHADOW SELF

Practice mindfulness and present moment awareness
when your shadow aspect arises. Observe its presence
without judgment or attachment. Write about any new
insights or observations you gain from this practice.

_____

_____

_____

_____

_____

_____

_____

_____

_____

_____

_____

Daily Check-in

DATE _____   S M T W T F

TODAY I APPRECIATE:

_____
_____
_____
_____
_____
_____
_____
_____

WATER IN TAKE:

△ △ △ △ △ △ △ △ △ △

MY FAVOURITE AFFIRMATIONS FOR TODAY:

_____
_____
_____
_____
_____
_____
_____

Day 18: Shadow Reflection

SELF-REFLECTION: GAZING INTO YOUR INNER SELF

Take a moment to look into the mirror and examine yourself from the outside and within. Pay attention to any emotions, opinions, or unease that arises. Take some time to jot down your observations and any ideas that emerge.

Self-reflection is an important part of personal growth and development. By taking the time to examine ourselves, we can gain a better understanding of who we are and what we want out of life. Looking into the mirror is a great way to start this process, as it allows us to see ourselves from an objective perspective. As you examine yourself, pay attention to any emotions that arise. Do you feel happy, sad, anxious, or excited? Try to identify the source of these emotions and explore them further. You may also notice certain opinions or beliefs about yourself that come up. Are these positive or negative? Consider where these opinions come from and whether they are serving you or holding you back. Finally, take note of any unease or discomfort that you feel. This could be a sign that something in your life needs to change or that you need to take better care of yourself. By taking the time to reflect on yourself in this way, you can gain valuable insights and make positive changes in your life.

Day 18: Shadow Reflection

SELF-REFLECTION: GAZING INTO YOUR INNER SELF

Find a mirror and look into your own eyes. Reflect on what you see, both externally and internally. Notice any emotions, judgments, or discomfort that arises. Write about your observations and any thoughts that come to the surface.

_____

_____

_____

_____

_____

_____

_____

_____

_____

_____

_____

_____

_____

_____

_____

_____

_____

_____

_____

_____

_____

_____

_____

_____

_____

_____

_____

Daily Check-in

DATE _____   S M T W T F

TODAY I APPRECIATE:

_____
_____
_____
_____
_____
_____
_____

WATER IN TAKE:

◊ ◊ ◊ ◊ ◊ ◊ ◊ ◊ ◊ ◊

MY FAVOURITE AFFIRMATIONS FOR TODAY:

_____
_____
_____
_____
_____
_____
_____

Day 19: Self-Compassionate Affirmations

Take some time to reflect on your shadow aspect and create a list of self-compassionate affirmations that cater to that part of you. Repeat these affirmations daily to remind yourself of your worth, progress, and growth. Make sure to jot them down for easy access.

By creating a list of self-compassionate affirmations that cater to our shadow aspect, we can begin to embrace our whole selves with love and kindness. These affirmations can help us to release any shame or guilt that we may feel about this part of ourselves, and instead focus on our worth, progress, and growth. By repeating these affirmations daily, we can remind ourselves of our inherent value and the progress we have made on our journey towards self-acceptance. So take some time to reflect on your shadow aspect and create those affirmations! Don't forget to jot them down for easy access so that you can remind yourself of your self-compassionate affirmations whenever you need them.

Remember that self-compassion is a crucial aspect of our overall well-being. It enables us to accept ourselves as we are, flaws and all, and to treat ourselves with the same kindness and understanding that we would offer to a dear friend. So, as you go through your day, try to be mindful of the ways in which you can show yourself compassion. Perhaps you can take a few deep breaths when you're feeling overwhelmed, or remind yourself that it's okay to make mistakes. Whatever it is, know that you are worthy of love and kindness, no matter what your shadow aspect may be. Keep practicing self-compassion, and you will find that it becomes easier and more natural over time.

Day 19: Self-Compassionate Affirmations

COMPILING A CATALOG OF SELF-COMPASSIONATE AFFIRMATIONS FOR YOUR SHADOW SELF

Create a list of self-compassionate affirmations specifically tailored to your shadow aspect. Use these affirmations as a daily reminder of your worthiness, growth, and progress. Write them down and repeat them daily.

_____

_____

_____

_____

_____

_____

_____

_____

_____

_____

_____

_____

Daily Check-in

DATE _____ S M T W T F

TODAY I APPRECIATE:

_____
_____
_____
_____
_____
_____
_____
_____

WATER IN TAKE:

◊ ◊ ◊ ◊ ◊ ◊ ◊ ◊ ◊ ◊

MY FAVOURITE AFFIRMATIONS FOR TODAY:

_____
_____
_____
_____
_____
_____
_____

Day 20: Release Ritual

CRAFTING A RELEASING RITUAL TO LET GO OF NEGATIVITY

If you're ready to bid farewell to your shadow qualities, consider creating a releasing ritual. Take a piece of paper and jot down what you want to let go of. Then, burn the paper and envision yourself being freed from those negative emotions. Reflect on the experience and write down any feelings of liberation you may have.

Creating a releasing ritual can be a powerful way to let go of negative emotions. It allows you to acknowledge the shadow qualities that may be holding you back and release them in a tangible way. Writing down what you want to let go of can help you identify these emotions and give them a name. Burning the paper can be a symbolic act of releasing them from your life. As you watch the paper burn, envision yourself being freed from those negative emotions and moving forward with a sense of clarity and purpose. Take some time to reflect on the experience and write down any feelings of liberation you may have. This can help solidify the ritual in your mind and serve as a reminder of the progress you've made. Remember, letting go of shadow qualities is a process, and it takes time and effort. But by creating a releasing ritual, you're taking an important step forward in your journey of self-discovery and growth.

Day 20: Release Ritual

CRAFTING A RELEASING RITUAL TO LET GO OF NEGATIVITY

Create a releasing ritual to symbolize your willingness to let go of your shadow quality. This could involve writing down what you're releasing, burning the paper, and visualizing the release. Write about the experience and any feelings of liberation.

_____

_____

_____

_____

_____

_____

_____

_____

_____

_____

_____

_____

Daily Check-in

DATE _____   S M T W T F

TODAY I APPRECIATE:

_____
_____
_____
_____
_____
_____
_____
_____

WATER IN TAKE:

◊ ◊ ◊ ◊ ◊ ◊ ◊ ◊ ◊ ◊

MY FAVOURITE AFFIRMATIONS FOR TODAY:

_____
_____
_____
_____
_____
_____
_____

Day 21: Journal Prompt Break

REFLECTING ON YOUR JOURNEY: SHADOW WORK WEEK THREE

Reflect on your shadow work journey so far and how it has impacted your self-awareness, self-acceptance, and growth.

_____

_____

_____

_____

_____

_____

_____

_____

_____

_____

_____

_____

Daily Check-in

DATE _____ S M T W T F

TODAY | APPRECIATE:

_____
_____
_____
_____
_____
_____
_____

WATER IN TAKE:

◊ ◊ ◊ ◊ ◊ ◊ ◊ ◊ ◊ ◊

MY FAVOURITE AFFIRMATIONS FOR TODAY:

_____
_____
_____
_____
_____
_____
_____

Day 22: Cultivating Self-Love

ENHANCE SELF-LOVE AND ACCEPTANCE THROUGH SHADOW WORK: SELF CARE PRACTICES AND ACTS OF KINDNESS

As you embark on your shadow work journey, there are ways to enrich your self-love and acceptance. Regularly implement self-care practices and acts of kindness to nurture and support yourself.

Additionally, try to approach your inner work with patience and compassion. Shadow work can be challenging and uncomfortable at times, but remember that you are doing important work to heal and grow. Take breaks as needed, and don't be too hard on yourself if you encounter resistance or setbacks.

It can also be helpful to seek support from trusted friends, family members, or a therapist. Having someone to talk to about your experiences can provide validation and encouragement along the way.

Above all, be gentle with yourself and remember that self-love and acceptance are ongoing practices. By committing to your shadow work journey and prioritizing your well-being, you can cultivate a deeper sense of self-awareness and inner peace.

Day 22: Cultivating Self-Love

ENHANCE SELF-LOVE AND ACCEPTANCE THROUGH SHADOW WORK:
SELF-CARE PRACTICES AND ACTS OF KINDNESS

Explore ways to deepen your self-love and acceptance throughout your shadow work journey. Write about self-care practices and acts of kindness you can implement regularly to nurture and support yourself.

_____

_____

_____

_____

_____

_____

_____

_____

_____

_____

_____

_____

Daily Check-in

DATE _____   S M T W T F

TODAY I APPRECIATE:

_____
_____
_____
_____
_____
_____
_____
_____

WATER IN TAKE:

◊ ◊ ◊ ◊ ◊ ◊ ◊ ◊ ◊ ◊

MY FAVOURITE AFFIRMATIONS FOR TODAY:

_____
_____
_____
_____
_____
_____
_____

Day 23: Empathy for Others

EXPLORING THE BENEFITS OF ACKNOWLEDGING YOUR SHADOW ASPECT

Take a moment to reflect on how acknowledging your shadow aspect can help you become more empathetic and understanding of those who have similar tendencies. Consider how this newfound empathy can improve your relationships and overall connection with others.

When we become aware of our own darker tendencies and accept them as a part of who we are, we can begin to recognize those same tendencies in others. This recognition can lead to greater understanding and compassion for those struggling with similar challenges. By acknowledging our own shadows, we can also become less judgmental of others, recognizing that we all have our own struggles and flaws.

This increased empathy and understanding can greatly benefit our relationships. Instead of being quick to judge or criticize, we can approach others with greater compassion and kindness. We may also find that we are better able to communicate with those around us, as we are more willing to listen and understand their perspective.

Overall, embracing our shadows can be a powerful tool for personal growth and improved relationships. By acknowledging our own imperfections and developing greater empathy for others, we can create a more compassionate and connected world.

Day 23: Empathy for Others

EXPLORING THE BENEFITS OF ACKNOWLEDGING YOUR SHADOW ASPECT

Reflect on how your shadow aspect allows you to be more empathetic and understanding towards others who may possess similar shadows. Write about how this newfound empathy can enhance your relationships and connection with others.

_____

_____

_____

_____

_____

_____

_____

_____

_____

_____

_____

_____

_____

Daily Check-in

DATE _____   S M T W T F

TODAY I APPRECIATE:

_____
_____
_____
_____
_____
_____
_____
_____

WATER IN TAKE:

◇ ◇ ◇ ◇ ◇ ◇ ◇ ◇ ◇ ◇

MY FAVOURITE AFFIRMATIONS FOR TODAY:

_____
_____
_____
_____
_____
_____
_____
_____

Day 24: Forgiving Others

EMBRACE FORGIVENESS TO OVERCOME YOUR SHADOW QUALITIES

Sometimes people have a significant impact on our lives, and not always for the best. If you're struggling with resentment or anger towards those who have triggered or contributed to your shadow qualities, try writing a letter of forgiveness. This can be a powerful way to let go of any negative emotions you're holding onto, freeing yourself up to move forward in a positive way.

Writing a forgiveness letter can be a daunting task, but it can also be a cathartic experience. Start by addressing the person you're writing to and acknowledge the hurt they caused you. Be honest about your feelings without blaming or criticizing them. Remember that forgiveness is not about excusing their behavior, but rather about releasing yourself from the burden of anger and hurt.

Next, try to put yourself in their shoes and understand their perspective. This doesn't mean you have to agree with them or condone their actions, but it can help you gain some perspective and empathy. Finally, express your forgiveness and let go of any resentment or negativity you may be holding onto.

It's important to remember that forgiveness is a process and it may not happen overnight. Be patient with yourself and allow yourself time to heal. You may find that writing multiple letters or revisiting the same letter over time can be helpful in letting go of negative emotions and finding peace.

Day 24: Forgiving Others

EMBRACE FORGIVENESS TO OVERCOME YOUR SHADOW QUALITIES

Practice forgiveness towards individuals who have triggered or played a role in shaping your shadow quality. Write a letter of forgiveness, expressing your willingness to let go of any resentment or anger attached to those experiences.

_____

_____

_____

_____

_____

_____

_____

_____

_____

_____

_____

_____

Daily Check-in

DATE _____   S M T W T F

TODAY I APPRECIATE:

_____
_____
_____
_____
_____
_____
_____
_____

WATER IN TAKE:

△ △ △ △ △ △ △ △ △ △

MY FAVOURITE AFFIRMATIONS FOR TODAY:

_____
_____
_____
_____
_____
_____
_____

Day 25: Shadow Alchemy

EMBRACING YOUR SHADOW SELF: TRANSFORMING WEAKNESS INTO STRENGTH

Discover the ways in which you can turn your shadow aspects into sources of strength and growth. Take some time to reflect on the qualities and traits that you can cultivate by accepting and integrating your shadow self.

Many of us have aspects of ourselves that we consider to be negative or undesirable. These aspects are often referred to as our "shadow self." However, rather than trying to suppress or ignore these qualities, it can be incredibly empowering to embrace and integrate them into our lives.

By acknowledging and accepting our shadow selves, we can unlock hidden sources of strength and creativity. For example, someone who struggles with anger may be able to channel that energy into fighting for justice and advocating for those who are marginalized. Similarly, someone who has a tendency towards self-doubt can use that vulnerability to connect with others and build authentic relationships.

Ultimately, the key to harnessing the power of your shadow self is to approach it with curiosity and compassion. Rather than judging yourself for your perceived flaws, try to view them as opportunities for growth and self-discovery. With time and practice, you may find that your shadow aspects become some of your greatest sources of strength and resilience.

Day 25: Shadow Alchemy

EMBRACING YOUR SHADOW SELF: TRANSFORMING WEAKNESS INTO STRENGTH

Explore how you can transform your shadow aspects into sources of strength and growth. Write about the qualities and traits that you can develop as a result of embracing and integrating your shadow self.

_____

_____

_____

_____

_____

_____

_____

_____

_____

_____

_____

Daily Check-in

DATE _____   S M T W T F

TODAY | APPRECIATE:

_____
_____
_____
_____
_____
_____
_____
_____

WATER IN TAKE:

◇ ◇ ◇ ◇ ◇ ◇ ◇ ◇ ◇ ◇

MY FAVOURITE AFFIRMATIONS FOR TODAY:

_____
_____
_____
_____
_____
_____
_____
_____

Day 26: Celebration of Integration

Take a moment to celebrate and acknowledge the progress you've made in integrating your shadow aspect. Write a letter to yourself, highlighting the growth, acceptance, and healing you've achieved through your shadow work.

Shadow work is a deeply personal journey that requires courage, vulnerability, and self-awareness. It's an ongoing process, and it's important to take a moment to acknowledge and celebrate the progress you've made so far.

In your letter, reflect on the ways in which you've grown through your shadow work. Perhaps you've learned to recognize and confront your negative thought patterns, or maybe you've developed a greater sense of compassion and empathy towards others. Whatever it may be, allow yourself to bask in the glow of your own achievements.

Remember to also highlight the acceptance you've cultivated towards your shadow aspects. Instead of suppressing or denying them, you've learned to embrace them as a part of your whole self. This acceptance has allowed you to integrate your shadow aspects into your conscious awareness, leading to greater emotional balance and inner peace.

Finally, acknowledge the healing that has taken place as a result of your shadow work. By confronting and working through your deepest wounds and fears, you've opened up space for growth, joy, and love in your life. Celebrate this healing and know that you are on the path to becoming the best version of yourself.

Day 26: Celebration of Integration

Celebrate and acknowledge the progress you have made in integrating your shadow aspect. Write a letter to yourself, recognizing the growth, acceptance, and healing achieved through your shadow work.

_____

_____

_____

_____

_____

_____

_____

_____

_____

_____

_____

_____

Daily Check-in

DATE _____   S M T W T F

TODAY I APPRECIATE:

_____
_____
_____
_____
_____
_____
_____

WATER IN TAKE:

⬭ ⬭ ⬭ ⬭ ⬭ ⬭ ⬭ ⬭ ⬭ ⬭

MY FAVOURITE AFFIRMATIONS FOR TODAY:

_____
_____
_____
_____
_____
_____
_____

Day 27: Reflection & Integration

Take a moment to reflect on the progress you've made during your shadow work journey. Consider writing about any transformations, lessons, or realizations that have arisen from this process. It's important to reflect on how you plan to continue incorporating your shadows into your life moving forward.

Reflecting on your journey can give you a better understanding of your own mind and emotions, and help you identify patterns and behaviors that might be holding you back. By acknowledging your shadows and working through them, you can cultivate greater self-awareness and create a more fulfilling life for yourself. Moving forward, it's important to continue to integrate your shadows into your daily life, whether it's through meditation, therapy, journaling, or other practices. Remember that shadow work is an ongoing process, and there's always room for growth and healing.

As you continue to incorporate your shadows into your life, it's important to approach this process with kindness and compassion for yourself. Understand that shadow work can be challenging and uncomfortable at times, but it's ultimately a necessary step towards healing and personal growth. Be patient with yourself and trust the process, knowing that each step you take towards integrating your shadows will bring you closer to a more authentic and fulfilling life. And always remember, you're not alone in this journey. There are many resources available to support you along the way, including therapists, support groups, and online communities. With dedication and commitment, you can continue to work through your shadows and create a brighter future for yourself.

Day 27: Reflection & Integration

Reflect on the overall impact of your shadow work journey. Write about any transformations, lessons, or realizations that have emerged during this process. Consider how you will continue to integrate your shadows moving forward.

_____

_____

_____

_____

_____

_____

_____

_____

_____

_____

_____

_____

Daily Check-in

DATE _____   S M T W T F

TODAY I APPRECIATE:

_____
_____
_____
_____
_____
_____
_____

WATER IN TAKE:

◇ ◇ ◇ ◇ ◇ ◇ ◇ ◇ ◇ ◇

MY FAVOURITE AFFIRMATIONS FOR TODAY:

_____
_____
_____
_____
_____
_____
_____

Day 28: Shadow Work Commitment

MAKING A LONG-TERM COMMITMENT TO SHADOW WORK

It's important to acknowledge the value of shadow work and commit to continuing it outside of your journal. To make a personal commitment, write a statement outlining your dedication to integrating your shadow self. Be specific about the actions you plan to take moving forward.

Shadow work is a process that can be challenging, but it's ultimately rewarding. By confronting and integrating the parts of ourselves that we've been avoiding or suppressing, we can experience a greater sense of wholeness and self-awareness. However, journaling alone isn't enough to fully integrate our shadow selves into our lives.

To truly commit to this work, we must make a conscious effort to apply what we've learned in our journals to our daily lives. This might mean seeking out therapy, talking to trusted friends or family members, or making new connections with people who share our interests and values. We might also need to set boundaries with people or situations that trigger our shadow selves, or practice self-compassion when we inevitably make mistakes.

Whatever actions we choose to take, it's crucial that we remain dedicated to the process. Shadow work isn't a one-time event, but an ongoing journey towards self-discovery and healing. By staying committed to this work, we can cultivate a deeper sense of self-awareness and compassion, both for ourselves and for others.

Day 28: Shadow Work Commitment

MAKING A LONG-TERM COMMITMENT TO SHADOW WORK

Recommit to continue your shadow work beyond this journal. Write a personal commitment statement outlining your dedication to embracing and integrating your shadow self. Include specific actions you will take moving forward.

_____

_____

_____

_____

_____

_____

_____

_____

_____

_____

_____

_____

Daily Check-in

DATE _____ S M T W T F

TODAY I APPRECIATE:

_____
_____
_____
_____
_____
_____
_____
_____

WATER IN TAKE:

○ ○ ○ ○ ○ ○ ○ ○ ○ ○

MY FAVOURITE AFFIRMATIONS FOR TODAY:

_____
_____
_____
_____
_____
_____
_____
_____

Day 29: Gratitude for the Journey

SHOWING APPRECIATION FOR THE TRANSFORMATIVE JOURNEY OF SHADOW WORK

Take time to reflect on the lessons learned and personal growth that this process has brought into your life. Create a gratitude list to acknowledge the positive impact it has had on your self-awareness.

The process of shadow work requires us to confront our deepest fears, insecurities, and negative patterns of behavior. It can be uncomfortable and sometimes painful, but the rewards are worth it. Through this process, we gain a deeper understanding of ourselves and our motivations. We learn to accept and integrate the parts of ourselves that we may have rejected or disowned in the past. This self-awareness allows us to navigate our lives with greater clarity and purpose. So, take some time to really appreciate the growth that you've experienced through shadow work. Write down all the ways in which this process has positively impacted your life, and don't forget to give yourself credit for the hard work you've done.

Day 29: Gratitude for the Journey

Express gratitude for the transformative journey of shadow work. Write a gratitude list, acknowledging the lessons learned, personal growth, and newfound self-awareness that this process has brought into your life.

_____

_____

_____

_____

_____

_____

_____

_____

_____

_____

Daily Check-in

DATE _____   S M T W T F

TODAY I APPRECIATE:

_____
_____
_____
_____
_____
_____
_____
_____

WATER IN TAKE:

◊ ◊ ◊ ◊ ◊ ◊ ◊ ◊ ◊ ◊

MY FAVOURITE AFFIRMATIONS FOR TODAY:

_____
_____
_____
_____
_____
_____
_____

Day 30: Shadow Work Reflection

TAKING A MOMENT TO REFLECT ON YOUR SHADOW WORK JOURNEY

It's time to take a step back and acknowledge the growth you've experienced in your shadow work journey. Take this opportunity to write a letter to yourself recapping the key insights, challenges, and moments of healing you've encountered. Remember to celebrate your progress and the courage it took to undertake this transformative process.

Shadow work can be an incredibly challenging and daunting process, but it can also be incredibly rewarding. By taking the time to reflect on your journey so far, you can gain a deeper understanding of yourself and the patterns that have been holding you back.

As you write your letter, don't be afraid to be honest and vulnerable with yourself. Acknowledge the difficult moments and the emotions that came up, but also celebrate the breakthroughs and moments of clarity that have helped you grow.

Remember that this is a journey, and there will be ups and downs along the way. But by taking the time to reflect on your progress, you can gain the strength and motivation to continue moving forward towards a more authentic and fulfilling life.

So take a deep breath, grab a pen and paper, and give yourself the gift of reflection and celebration. You deserve it!

Day 30: Shadow Work Reflection

Reflect on your complete shadow work journey. Write a letter to yourself, summarizing the key insights, challenges, and moments of healing and growth you experienced. Celebrate yourself for embracing this transformative process.

_____

_____

_____

_____

_____

_____

_____

_____

_____

_____

_____

_____

Conclusion

Completing your 30-day shadow work journal is a big accomplishment! However, always remember that shadow work is a lifelong journey, and every day is an opportunity for growth and self-discovery. Keep exploring and embracing your shadow self with empathy, inquisitiveness, and a dedication to personal healing and integration.

As you continue on your journey, it's important to remember that shadow work isn't always easy. You may encounter difficult emotions or memories that you've been avoiding. But don't give up. Through facing your shadows, you'll gain a deeper understanding of yourself, and you'll be able to heal and grow in ways you never thought possible.

Remember to be kind to yourself throughout the process. It's okay to take breaks and to give yourself time to process your emotions. You don't have to rush through your shadow work. Take your time and allow yourself to fully experience the journey.

Finally, know that you're not alone. There are many resources available to help you along the way, including therapists, support groups, and online communities. Don't hesitate to reach out for help when you need it.

With dedication and compassion, you can continue to explore and embrace your shadow self, leading to a more fulfilling and authentic life.

Made in United States
Troutdale, OR
01/23/2024

17076481R00066